THIS JOURNAL BELONGS TO:

_____

BORN: _____   PLACE OF BIRTH: _____

ENTRY DATE: _____   AGE: _____

ENTRY DATE: _____   AGE: _____

ENTRY DATE: _____   AGE: _____

DIED:

_____

OTHER BOOKS BY THE AUTHOR

Sophia and Pepe's Adventure Series

Sofia's Awesome Tamale Day
The Search for the Lost Art of Making Tortillas
Isabela's Treasure
Sofia's Summer Adventure
Sofia's Awesome Tamale Day (Spanish Edition)

Historical Memoir

Better Than Me: Three Generations of Inner Strength

Find all of Albert's books on **Amazon.com**,
or visit his website at **albertmonrealquihuis.com**,
or contact him at **aquihuis@msn.com**.

THE LEGACY JOURNAL

THE LEGACY JOURNAL

A Treasure Map to Your Life and Heritage

Authored by

ALBERT MONREAL QUIHUIS

Published by
Albert Monreal Quihuis
© 2020

The Legacy Journal
A Treasure Map to Your Life and Heritage
©2020 Albert Monreal Quihuis

Published by Albert Monreal Quihuis
Chandler, AZ

ISBN: 9798553980818 (paperback)

Library of Congress Control Number: 2020921362

Cover and interior design Grace Quest, thegracequest@gmail.com

Book Shepherd, Ann Narcisian Videan, ANVidean.com

This book is dedicated to
those who came to our land long ago
and made it their home…
our ancestors.

They faced the unknown,
hungered, and toiled.
Their endurance and struggles
are our prosperity.

We are forever grateful.

CONTENTS

PREFACE

One summer day in my youth, my family went on a day trip to visit San Xavier del Bac, a Historic Spanish Mission. Called "The White Dove of the Desert," it lies ten miles south of Tucson, Arizona. As we neared the mission, I saw an elderly man wearing an old cowboy hat sitting underneath a shady mesquite tree. He appeared deep in thought staring at the mission and the Sonoran Desert. Maybe he was resting, waiting for a ride, enjoying the scenery, or reflecting on his life. As we drove closer, I was able to look upon his face. It showed that this man had lived a long hard life. It made me wonder what would happen to this man's hard-earned experiences, knowledge, wisdom, memories, secrets, and loves. How would he be remembered when he passed on? Would he be able to reveal this information to his family and grandchildren? What about stories and memories of his parents, grandparents, and his ancestors? Would he be able to write their stories, or does the legacy vanish with the wind?

If you could time travel to the past and visit an ancestor, what would you ask, what would you want to know?

If you could time travel to the future and visit your descendants, what would you want them to know about you and about your family legacy?

This book offers the opportunity to travel and create a written legacy for all generations, past, present, and future.

INTRODUCTION

During my life journey of writing, speaking, and becoming an award-winning author, I have come to realize all my books carry an underlying theme of honoring our ancestors for their determination and hard work to give us a better life. My books have stirred readers' memories and inspired them to write stories of *their* ancestors so they are not forgotten. Documenting your family history keeps memories alive and allows future generations to know who they are and where they came from. Knowing and understanding their circumstances creates a sense of pride and self-worth.

Most ancestry programs encourage you to start researching and documenting the past, your parents, and ancestors. *The Legacy Journal* encourages this, too, but starts in the present, visualizing the future with the person who you are most familiar with… yourself. It may be hard to visualize that, many generations from now, your stories, beliefs, and values will have interest and purpose for your bloodline, but they will. It may be heartwarming to know your descendants will learn from your experiences and take pride in the many things they share in common.

Use this journal to start the process—to write/rewrite, search/research, and locate documents, records, and old pictures. Start by marking on the following map where you and your family members have lived over the decades. Can you add cities, dates, or other information to provide an even more detailed account? As you move forward, you do not need to answer every question—add, delete, insert, change, or just think about it. Fill the space on the journal's odd pages with any overflow writing, new ideas, lists, important papers, stories, art, photos, and more. We've even left a space on the book's spine for you to ink in your initials and dates so individuals' journals are easy to locate on a bookshelf.

Instead of each generation trying to piece together unorganized fragments of stories, pictures, and timelines; and feeling bewildered as they attempt to recreate your family legacy; they will have personal documentation of each individual's story in that generation. Your journals should be passed down to the next generation's members so each of them can create their own journals to pass on to their respective descendants. As the years march on, your family will treasure the long line of documented family history, with no more wondering and guessing.

Later, you can learn more about your ancestors and the world events that influenced their lives through external resources: DNA testing, genealogy research, the family tree, and downloading ancestry applications.

This is the adventure of many lifetimes. Weave your stories and be the first to create a beautiful journal for your family, celebrating life with pride,

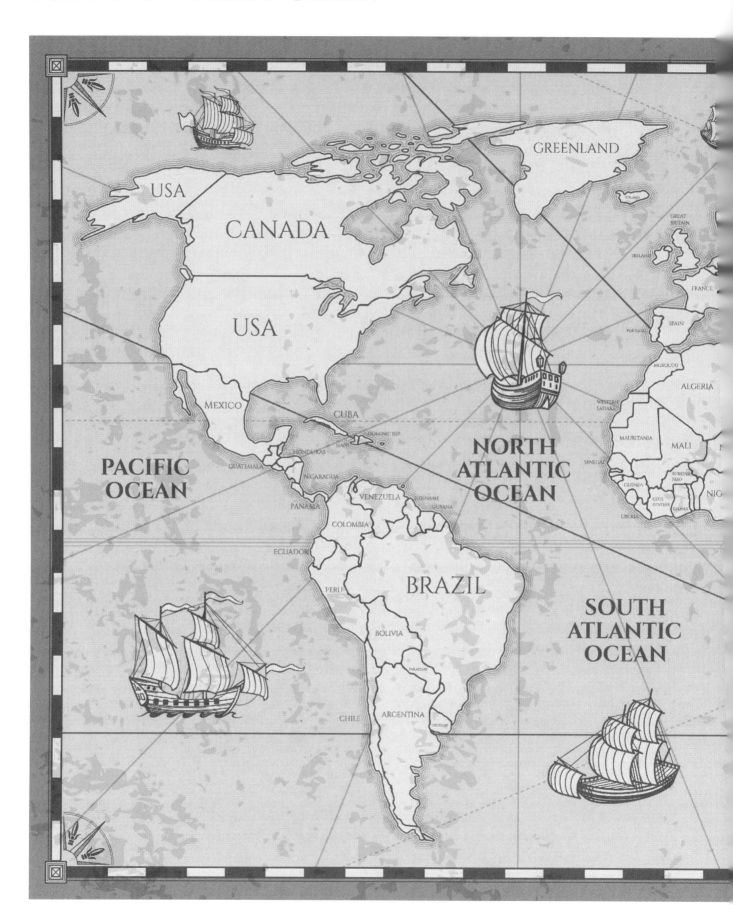

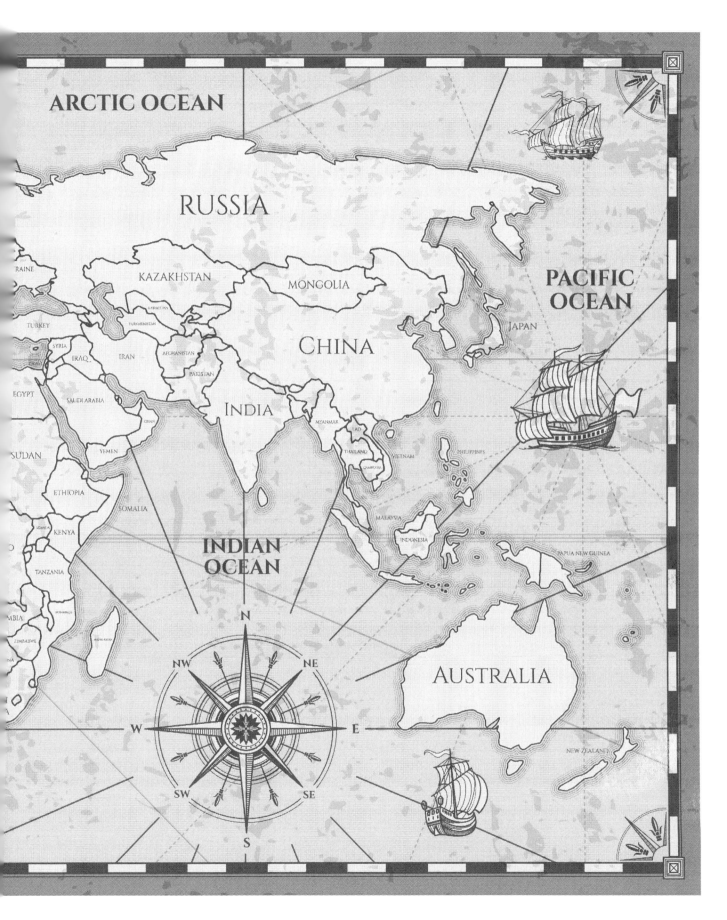

ARCTIC OCEAN

RUSSIA

KAZAKHSTAN

MONGOLIA

PACIFIC
OCEAN

UZBEKISTAN

TURKEY

TURKMENISTAN

JAPAN

SYRIA

IRAQ

IRAN

AFGHANISTAN

CHINA

EGYPT

SAUDI ARABIA

PAKISTAN

OMAN

INDIA

MYANMAR

SUDAN

YEMEN

LAO

ETHIOPIA

THAILAND

VIETNAM

PHILIPPINES

SOMALIA

CAMBODIA

KENYA

INDIAN
OCEAN

MALAYSIA

TANZANIA

INDONESIA

PAPUA NEW GUINEA

ZAMBIA

MADAGASCAR

ZIMBABWE

N

NW

NE

AUSTRALIA

W

E

NEW ZEALAND

SW

SE

S

PERSONAL
HISTORY

SECTION I:
ALL ABOUT YOU

1. What is your full name, maiden name, nicknames?

2. How/why did they pick your name, nicknames?

3. Date of birth, time, day of the week, location, weather?

4. Write about your parents/guardians.

What else can you share?

5. Your first memory?

6. Number of siblings? What number are you?

7. Write about your siblings? Names, quirks, favorite memories?

8. What are the names of your, past or present, spouse(s) or significant other(s)

_____

_____

_____

9. Do you have children, grandchildren, and/or great-grandchildren?
If yes, how many? What are their names?

_____

_____

_____

10. Places you lived?

_____

_____

_____

11. First language? Other spoken languages?

_____

_____

12. Favorite toys, games, activities?

_____

_____

_____

13. Did you enjoy playing inside, outside, daytime, nighttime? What games did you play?

14. Names of pets and friends?

15. Special memories while growing up?

16. Memories of your birthday?

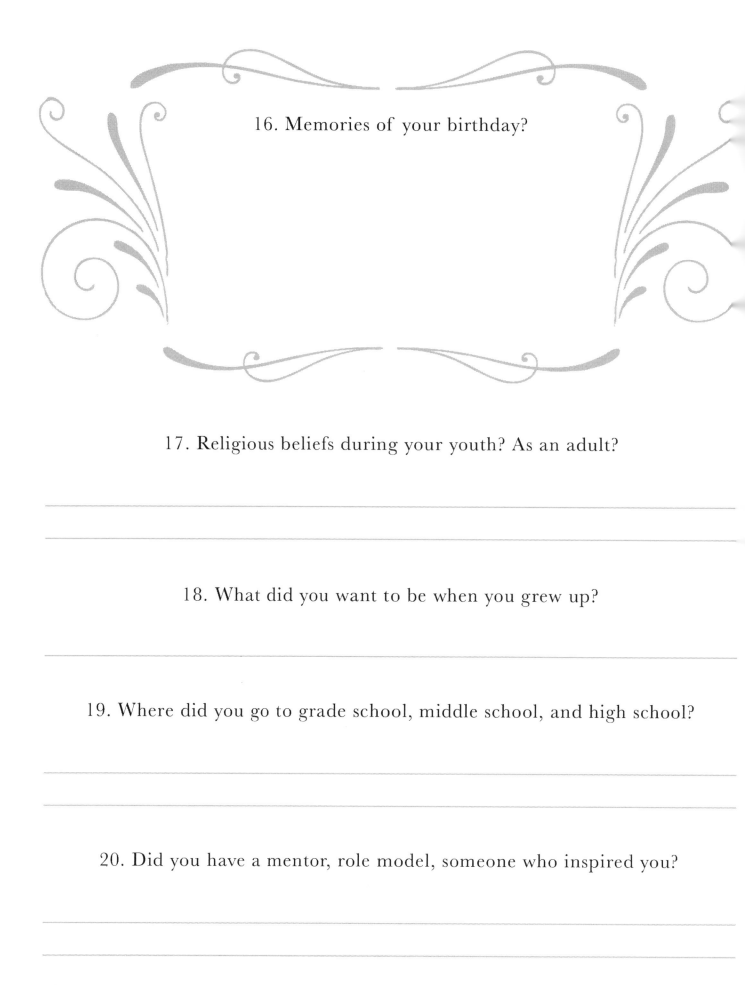

17. Religious beliefs during your youth? As an adult?

18. What did you want to be when you grew up?

19. Where did you go to grade school, middle school, and high school?

20. Did you have a mentor, role model, someone who inspired you?

21. Favorite subjects, teachers, activities, school memories?

22. Where did you attend trade school(s), college(s), higher education? What degree(s)/certification(s) did you achieve, if applicable?

23. When did you first leave home? Write about the experience.

24. What was your first job? Your favorite job?

_____

_____

25. What type of careers have you worked in?

_____

_____

26. Did/do you serve in the military? In what capacity?
Highlights from your experience?

_____

_____

_____

27. Are you or were you a member of any clubs, organizations, and associations?

_____

_____

28. Have you received recognitions, certificates, awards, medals?

_____

_____

29. What special skills do you possess?

_____

_____

_____

30. What was your favorite sport to play or watch? Favorite athletic teams?

_____

_____

31. What are your hobbies and interests?

_____

_____

_____

_____

32. You are:

☐ Introverted
☐ Extroverted

33. You are:

☐ A Leader
☐ A Follower
☐ A Free Spirit

34. You are:

☐ Right-handed
☐ Left-handed

35. You prefer:

☐ Sunrise
☐ Sunset
☐ Both

36. What is your favorite color?

37. What is your blood type? Do you donate blood?

38. Color of your hair? Eyes? Skin Tone?

39. How tall are you?

40. Do you wear glasses or contacts?

41. Size of your shoes? Ring size? Hat size?

42. Do you have hereditary health issues? Allergies?

43. Have you had any notable illnesses and/or injuries?

_____

_____

_____

_____

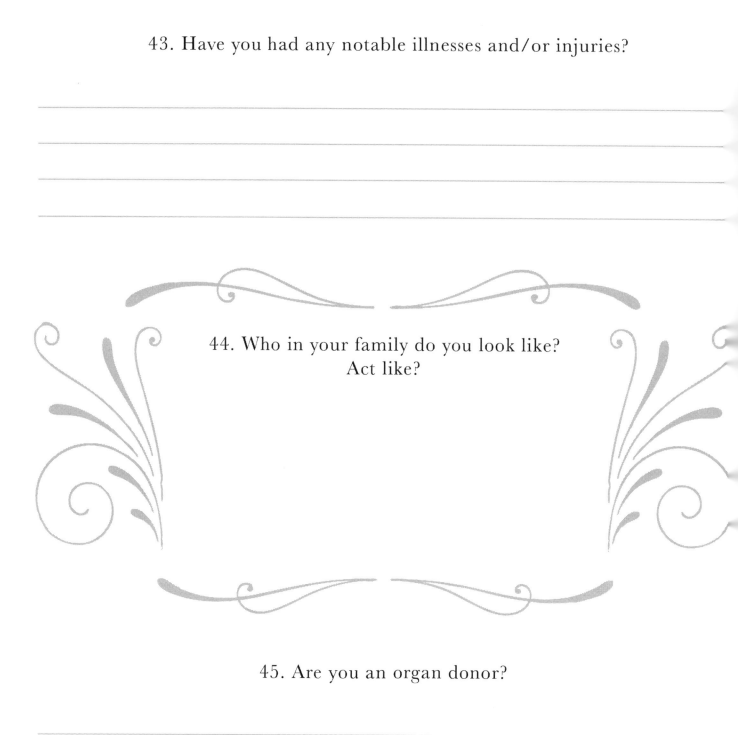

44. Who in your family do you look like?
Act like?

45. Are you an organ donor?

_____

SECTION II:
WHAT YOU LIKE

46. What's on your bucket list?

What else can you share?

47. Favorite vacations, road trips, tours, and/or cruises?

48. Favorite places you have visited?

49. Favorite historical sites, national parks, museums, or UNESCO World Heritage Sites?

50. Favorite way to travel?

51. You know how to:

☐ Swim   ☐ Ride a bike
☐ Ski   ☐ Ride a motorcycle
☐ Climb a tree ☐ Ride a horse
☐ Somersault

52. On your vacations, you prefer

☐ Camping
☐ Hotels
☐ Staying with friends/relatives
☐ Traveling in an RV

53. Do you enjoy creating art? Are you creative?

54. Can you sing, whistle, or play an instrument?

55. Favorite style of dance? Who is your favorite dance partner?

56. Favorite movies, television shows, musicals, plays, and actors?

_____

_____

_____

_____

57. Favorite books, fiction, nonfiction, self-help, and authors?

_____

_____

_____

_____

58. Favorite kind of music, instrument, songs, singers, bands, orchestra?

_____

_____

_____

_____

59. Favorite style of clothes, shoes, hats, or jewelry? Formal or casual?

_____

_____

_____

_____

60. Favorite activities during:

Spring	Summer	Autumn	Winter

61. Favorite holidays: national, cultural, and/or religious?

62. Do you like to cook, grill, bake, or microwave? What is your specialty? Special holiday meals? Favorite family recipes?

63. Favorite foods and beverages? Favorite dessert?

64. Favorite animals on land, in the sky, and in the sea?

65. Favorite flower, plant, and tree?

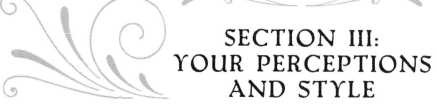

SECTION III:
YOUR PERCEPTIONS AND STYLE

66. At events and parties do you arrive early, on time, or late? Do you make a grand entrance or come in quietly?

67. Who are your best friends? What friend always has your back?

68. Best exercise tips for staying healthy?

69. Best eating tips for staying healthy?

70. Best tips for being healthy, wealthy, and wise?

71. Best advice for living a fulfilling life?

72. What is your passion?

73. Do you find technology to be challenging or do you embrace it?

74. Do you like change?

75. Do you dream? In color? Do you have the same recurring dream? Do your dreams have meaning?

76. Do you meditate, pray, self-reflect, and/or practice moments of silence?

77. Do you believe in karma?

78. Saddest memory?

79. Happiest memory?

80. Funniest things that happened to you? Most embarrassing moments?

_____

_____

_____

_____

81. Biggest surprise of your life?

_____

_____

_____

82. The most important events in your life?

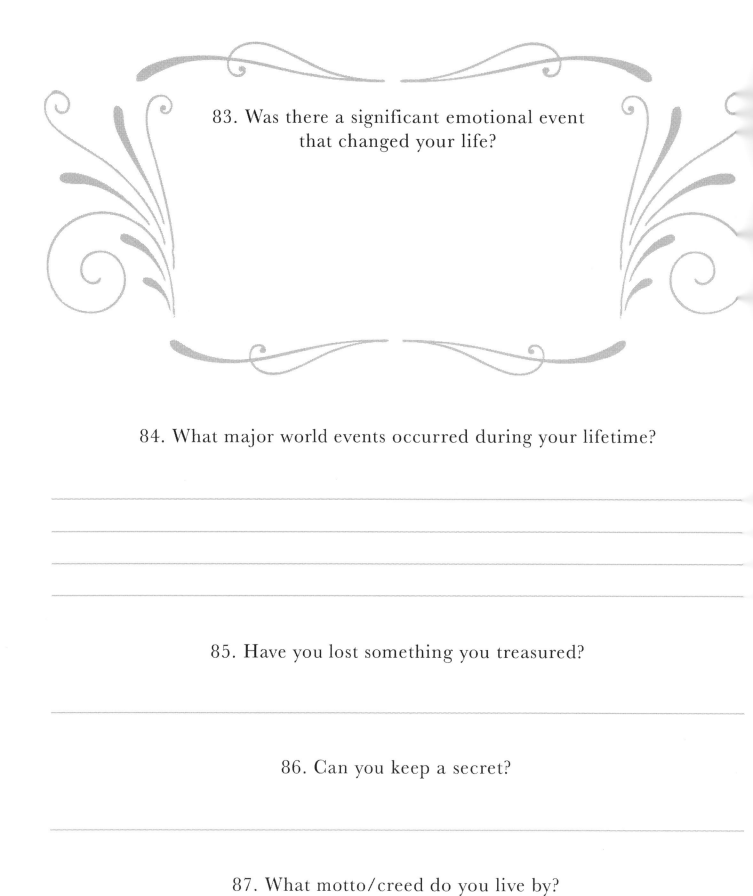

83. Was there a significant emotional event
that changed your life?

84. What major world events occurred during your lifetime?

_____

_____

_____

_____

85. Have you lost something you treasured?

_____

86. Can you keep a secret?

_____

87. What motto/creed do you live by?

_____

SECTION IV:
YOUR EXISTENTIAL
QUALITIES & BELIEFS

88. If you won the lottery what would you do?

89. If a genie granted you three wishes, what would they be?

1.
2.
3.

90. If your house caught fire what would you save?

91. Do you believe in ghosts, spirits, and the afterlife?

What else can you share?

92. Do you believe in aliens, spaceships, and flying saucers?

93. Have you had a supernatural and/or out of body experience?

94. Do you have a sixth sense, and are you clairvoyant?

95. Do you believe in time travel, past lives, reincarnation, or other dimensions?

96. Do you have fears, phobias, or superstitions?

97. Do you have a special item or good luck charm you carry with you?

98. Have you, or would you:

Skydive?

☐ I have ☐ I would

Ride in a hot air balloon?

☐ I have ☐ I would

Bungee jump?

☐ I have ☐ I would

Zip line?

☐ I have ☐ I would

Pilot a plane?

☐ I have ☐ I would

99. Would you board a flying saucer, knowing you might not come back?

100. If you were stranded on an island, what would be your choice of food, drink, and tool to survive?

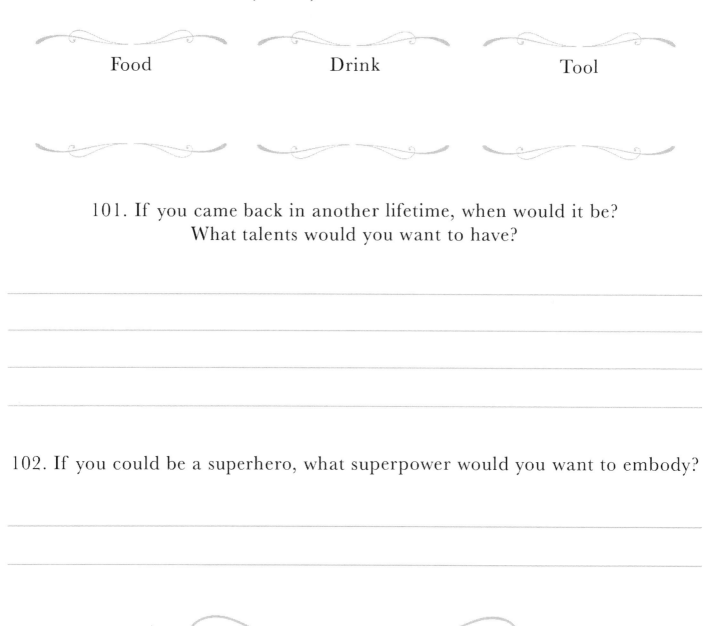

Food   Drink   Tool

101. If you came back in another lifetime, when would it be? What talents would you want to have?

102. If you could be a superhero, what superpower would you want to embody?

103. Which historical figure would you like to meet?

104. If you had to live your life again, what would you do differently?

105. Did you ever make New Year's resolutions?

106. What were some daily and lifetime goals?

107. What accomplishments are you most proud of?

108. What were your biggest challenges?

109. Have you ever been the target of prejudice?

110. What are your greatest strengths and weaknesses?

111. What words of faith or wisdom do you live by?

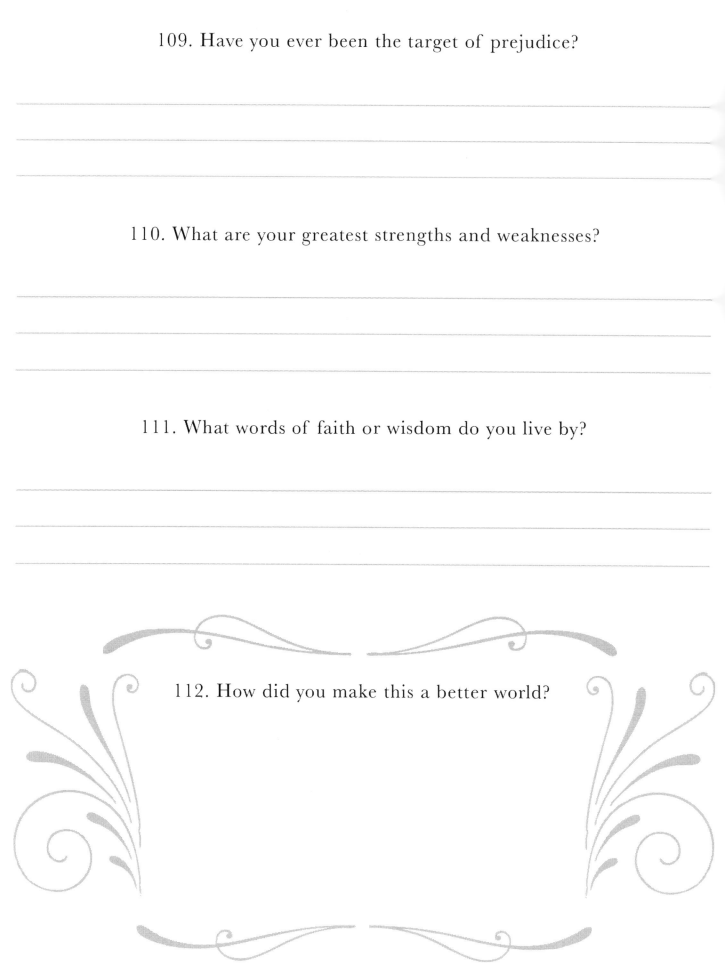

112. How did you make this a better world?

113. What did you try to teach your children?

114. What did your children teach you?

115. The greatest lessons you learned?

116. Share one thing nobody knows about you.

117. You forgive... whom?

118. Your greatest love? Soul mate? Secret loves?

119. What should be engraved on your headstone?

120. What question was left out that you would like
to ask yourself and answer?

121. What did you learn about yourself in completing this project?

ANCESTRAL
HISTORY

SECTION I:
ALL ABOUT YOUR ANCESTORS

1. Parents' names, maiden names, nicknames, dates of births, deaths?

_____

_____

_____

_____

2. Where did your parents come from? What language(s) did they speak? Did they receive an education?

_____

_____

_____

_____

3. Where did your parents meet? Where did they get married?

_____

_____

_____

_____

What else can you share?

4. What jobs or careers did your parents have?
Special memories?

5. Any awards your parents received?

6. Did your parents ever experience illnesses and injuries?

7. Write about your aunts, uncles, and cousins.

8. Grandparents' names, maiden names, nicknames, dates of births, deaths?

9. Where did your grandparents come from? What language(s) did they speak? Did they receive an education?

10. Where did your grandparents meet? Where did they get married?

11. What jobs or careers did your grandparents have?
Special memories?

12. Write about your great-aunts and great-uncles?

13. Great-grandparents' names, maiden names, dates of births, deaths?

14. Where did your great-grandparents come from?
What language(s) did they speak? Did they receive an education?

_____

_____

_____

_____

_____

15. Where did your great-grandparents meet? Where did they get married?

_____

_____

_____

_____

_____

16. What jobs or careers did your great-grandparents have?
Special memories?

17. Do you have family names? What's the origin, meaning, ethnic group, country, language, and/or time period?

18. Is your family royalty? Do they have a coat of arms, family crest flag, colors, treasure chests, hidden treasures, etc.?

19. Famous ancestor or distant relatives? Infamous family members, history, unique stories, and lore that have been passed down?

20. Lost, missing, or forgotten family members?

_____
_____
_____
_____

21. Is there a person, or people, who are not blood related
yet you consider to be family?

_____
_____
_____
_____

22. Are there family secrets you want to reveal here?

_____
_____
_____
_____

23. Did anyone in your family serve in the military? In what branch of service,
war, revolution, and/or assigned countries did they serve?

_____
_____
_____
_____

SECTION II:
ANCESTORS' INFLUENCE
AND LEGACY

24. What values and beliefs have your ancestors passed down?

25. Family words of wisdom you live by?

26. How do you honor the hard work and sacrifices
of your ancestors to give you a better life?

27. How has your family legacy made you proud of who you are?

What else can you share?

28. How has your family legacy inspired and made you a better person?

_____

_____

_____

_____

29. How do you want your family legacy to be remembered?

_____

_____

_____

_____

30. What questions would you want to ask your ancestors?

31. What would you want your ancestors to know about you?

32. What do you want your descendants to know about you?

33. How do you think you will be remembered?

34. How do you want to be remembered?

35. Your most treasured family traditions?

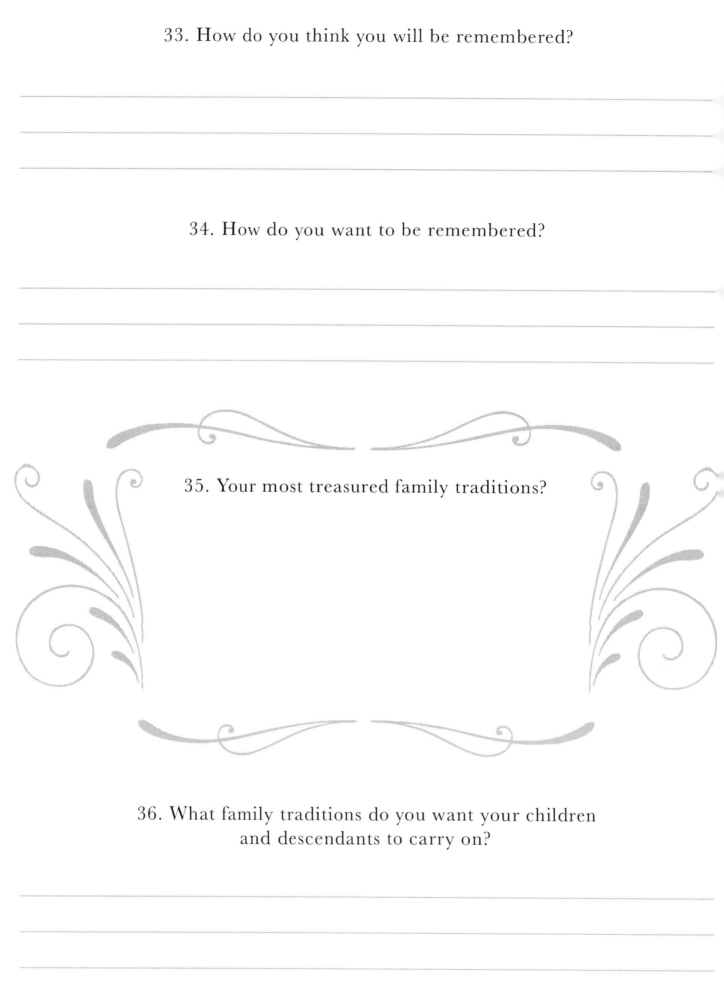

36. What family traditions do you want your children
and descendants to carry on?

37. What advice would you give for safeguarding *The Legacy Journals* completed by you, and all future family?

38. What will be your famous last words?

ACTIVITIES

- Create a family tree and/or ancestor timeline.

- Sketch a map of your childhood neighborhood, school, family farm/ranch, etc.

- Compile favorite quotes, proverbs, poems, songs, stories, scriptures, etc.

- Ask friends and relatives to write their favorite story about you.

- Look through, and/or attach, letters and photos.

- Look over records, documents, deeds, land grants, mining claims, treasure maps, etc.

- Find antiques, collectibles, and/or heirlooms.

- Invest in DNA information and genealogy research.

- Make and bury a time capsule.

- Write your epitaph

RESEARCH SOURCES

- Attics: look for old trunks, chests, and boxes
- Bible records
- Birth and death records
- Cemetery records and obituaries
- Church records
- Census records
- County and state records
- Directories, phone books, and organizations
- Divorce records
- Letters, labeled backs of photos, diaries, journals, and personal communications
- Marriage records
- Military records
- Naturalizations
- Newspapers
- Trade unions
- Wills, trusts, deeds

YOUR MESSAGE
TO FAMILY

Use the following pages to write a note(s) to your family as a whole,
to a few individuals, or one person. Think about including what you'd
like them to most remember about you, share some invaluable knowledge
or hopes for them, and/or predict how you envision the family unfolding
in the future. This is your space to speak directly to your loved ones and
share your most poignant thoughts.

REQUEST FOR REVIEW

If you enjoyed this book, please consider
leaving a review about it on Albert Monreal Quihuis'
book page on Amazon.com.

ABOUT THE AUTHOR

Albert Monreal Quihuis is a multiple award-winning author, a presenter, Arizona Historian, educator and Hispanic Community Advocate. He wrote his first children's book to honor his parents and family traditions. At that time, he realized the need for multicultural books and became passionate about writing books to motivate and inspire children to learn about their traditions, culture, history, and feel pride in their heritages.

He reads aloud in schools, libraries, and museums; and gives presentations to educators, writers, and organizations. In 2018, he published *Better Than Me*, his first young-adult book, which most adults show interest in as well. Currently, he is writing and researching several historical novels and continues to write the next book in his *Sofia and Pepe the Parrot* Adventure Series.

A native of Arizona, Albert can trace ancestors in the state back to the 1700s. He graduated from Arizona State University and is a veteran of the United States Air Force.

Contact Albert at aquihuis@msn.com.

Made in United States
Troutdale, OR
06/06/2024